F is for Foreword

F is for foreword … and fantastic, and family, and friends, and fabulous. We are thrilled to thank our fantastic family and friends who did such a fabulous job helping us reach our Kickstarter goal to produce this book. This list reflects those who helped or the people and places they have chosen to honor.

Abby & Isabella O'Connor
Alvin & Phyllis Katz
Amy B.
Ann & Roger Cole
Betty & Steve Westrope
David Conners
David "Riceman" Sessions
Ed Padala
Edward R. & Patricia Padala
Ian Bearman & Jennifer Dinges
Joe's House, a lodging guide for cancer patients

John Gallagher
Josiah Warren
Julie & Larry Gelb
Karen Wylie
Mary & Vivek
Matt, Tia, Chris & Jim Boyle
Scott & Karen Burstein
Sofia Forte
The Metzger/Strecker Family
The Sallenave Family
Wenli

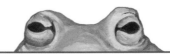

Animal Store Alphabet Book
Text © 2012 by Susan Bearman
Illustrations © 2012 by Rebecca Hamlin

ISBN 978-0-9885785-0-0

Library of Congress Control Number: 2012920890

Published in the United States by

Orrington Press
Evanston, Illinois
orringtonpress.com

Address all inquiries to
asab@orringtonpress.com
Reseller discounts available.

Teaching tools and more available at
alphabetanimal.com

Printed by Book Printing Revolution, Minnesota / USA

Animal Store Alphabet Book

Susan Bearman
words

Rebecca Hamlin
pictures

orrington press

To K.I.B.I.M.N.S., because you're all that really matters.
With special thanks to Rebecca and EJP.

Susan

To Robert, Sam and Ari for their love and support, and for
sharing their home with this book for such a long time.

Rebecca

Welcome to the Animal Store
Where this is what you'll see
The "who-knew zoo" just down the street
With pets from A-Z.

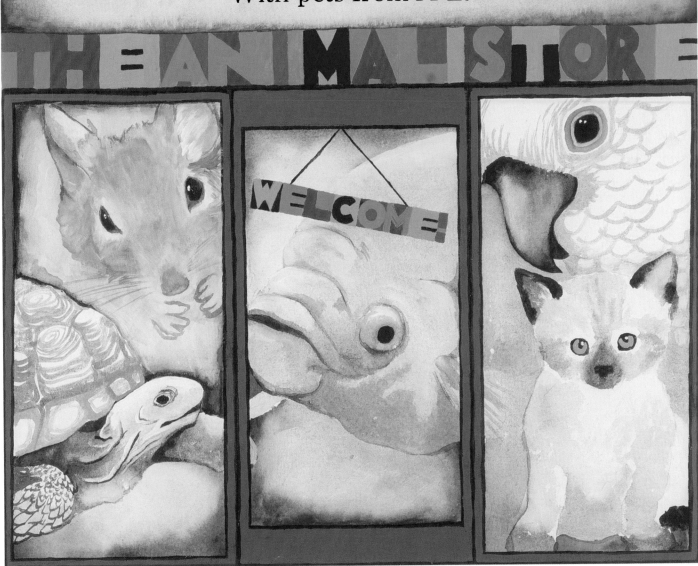

Salamanders, newts, toads and frogs are all Amphibians.

Amphibians seem
quite confused
They don't know
where to dwell

First in water,
then on land
Their webbed feet
serve them well.

Amphibians can breathe through their skin.

Baby Amphibians (tadpoles) are born in water and look like small fish.

A is for Amphibian

A Bearded Dragon's chin puffs out and turns black to ward off predators.

Beardies can run on their hind legs.

Lightning bugs are poisonous to Bearded Dragons.

The Bearded Dragon
breathes no fire
She is a gentle beast

She puffs her spiky chin to prove
She's not scared in the least.

B is for Bearded Dragon

Corals are small animals related to jellyfish and anemone.

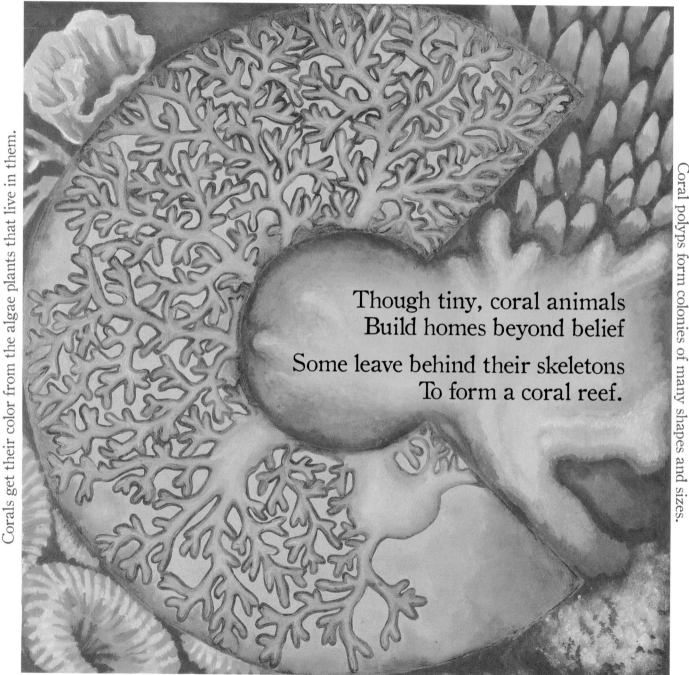

Corals get their color from the algae plants that live in them.

Coral polyps form colonies of many shapes and sizes.

Though tiny, coral animals
Build homes beyond belief

Some leave behind their skeletons
To form a coral reef.

C is for Coral

A Degu looks like a large gerbil with a bushy tuft at the end of its tail.

Degu is strange,
his teeth are orange
As if they've
turned to rust

He never takes
a bubble bath
A Degu bathes
in dust.

A healthy Degu has orange front teeth.

Degus take dust baths to clean and protect their fur and skin.

D is for Degu

Eclectus Parrots are great mimics.

Female Eclectus Parrots are bright red and purple/blue.

Male Eclectus Parrots are vibrant green with red under feathers.

Colorful Eclectus Parrots
Wear green and red and blue

So clever, they can learn to talk
And have a chat with you.

E is for Eclectus Parrot

The word "Ferret" comes from the Latin word for thief.

The frisky Ferret runs and romps
He'll squeeze beneath your door

Then hide his toys and
steal your socks
A rascal to the core.

Ferrets can be litter trained.

Ferrets have flexible bones that let them fit through tight spaces.

F is for Ferret

A Guinea Pig can jump straight up in the air when happy or excited.

Every Guinea Pig has five different types of fur.

Guinea Pigs are very social and bond well with their human family and other pets.

The Guinea Pig is
not a pig
Really, it's a cavy

Some have short hair,
some have long and
Some are soft and wavy.

G is for Guinea Pig

Hedgehogs roll into a ball to protect their soft bellies.

Pygmy Hedgehogs are smart and have good memories.

A Hedgehog's quills are sharp, but not barbed.

The Hedgehog is a ball of quills
Whenever he's upset

But he's a softy underneath
A friendly, playful pet.

H is for Hedgehog

The green Iguana's scientific name is *Iguana iguana*.

If an Iguana loses its tail, it can grow a new one.

The green Iguana's
quite a jock
He'll run and
swim and climb

He also likes
to bob his head
And wave from
time to time.

The fold of skin under the Iguana's chin is called a dewlap.

I is for Iguana

Jungle Pythons are constrictors, which means they squeeze their prey.

Pythons use S-shaped movements on land and in water to propel themselves forward.

A Jungle Python's born
so small
Yet everyone agrees

When she's full grown,
you never want
To give this snake a squeeze.

A full-grown Jungle Python will reach three to six feet in length.

J is for Jungle Carpet Python

Kittens and cats have been kept as pets for more than 9,500 years.

A Kitten has
such energy
He'll caper,
pounce
and leap

A group of kittens is called a litter or a kindle.

All kittens are born with blue eyes, which may change color as they get older.

But look again,
he's tuckered out
And fallen fast asleep.

K is for Kitten

Lovebirds are small members of the parrot family.

Lovebirds like to preen (or groom) one another.

While Lovebirds look cute together, single birds bond better with humans.

Two Lovebirds snuggled on their perch
Make such a cozy pair

They groom each other every day
With tender loving care.

L is for Lovebird

Millipede means "thousand legs", but most species have fewer than 200.

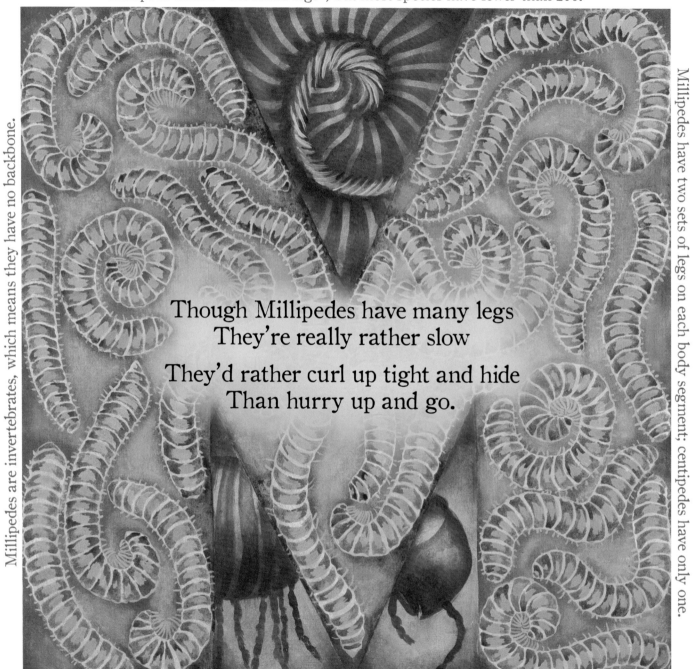

Millipedes are invertebrates, which means they have no backbone.

Millipedes have two sets of legs on each body segment; centipedes have only one.

Though Millipedes have many legs
They're really rather slow

They'd rather curl up tight and hide
Than hurry up and go.

M is for Millipede

Nile Monitors can stay under water for more than an hour.

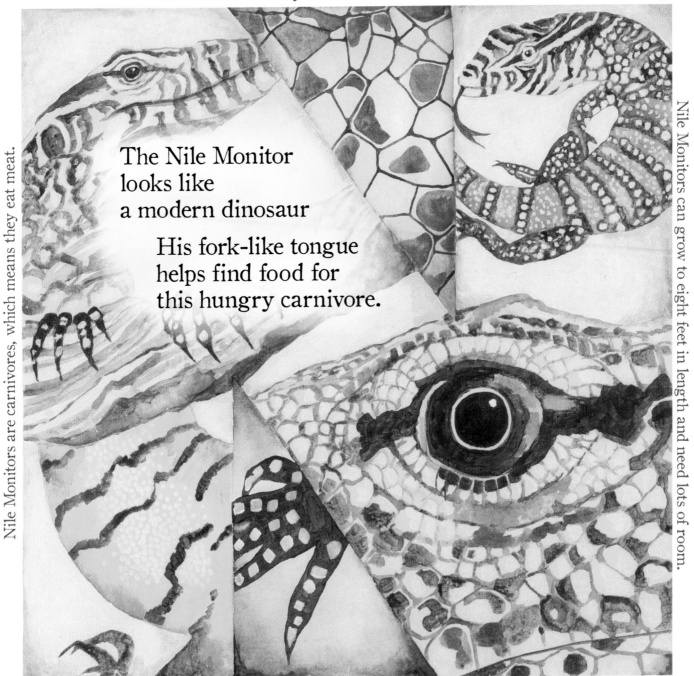

Nile Monitors are carnivores, which means they eat meat.

Nile Monitors can grow to eight feet in length and need lots of room.

The Nile Monitor
looks like
a modern dinosaur

His fork-like tongue
helps find food for
this hungry carnivore.

N is for Nile Monitor

The telltale bump, or hood, on the Oranda's head is called a wen.

The Chinese call the Oranda "flower of the water".

Orandas come in a variety of color combinations and calicos.

Oranda wears
a fancy hat
So beautiful
and chic

Exotic veils for fins
and tails
Make this
goldfish unique.

O is for Oranda

Short-tailed Pygmy Opossums are pouchless marsupials.

The Pygmy Opossum
lives alone
She loves to run and climb

Asleep all day,
at play all night
She lives in backward time.

Male Pygmy Opossums are called jacks, females are jills.

Pygmy Opossums are nocturnal, which means they're awake at night.

P is for Pygmy Opossum

Quakers are also known as monk parrots or parakeets.

Quakers are the only parrots that build their own nests.

Quakers are good talkers; only African grey parrots are better.

A Quaker can be comical
His antics are a treat

And when he shakes from head to tail
You'll know he wants to eat.

Q is for Quaker Parakeet

A female Rabbit is a doe, a male is a buck (just like deer).

A rabbit's 28 teeth never stop growing.

Rabbits can turn their ears in any direction.

The Rabbit wants to dig
and chew
She often likes to doze

She shows her
curiosity
By wiggling
her nose.

R is for Rabbit

Scorpions have been on earth for more than 400 million years.

Scorpions can have up to five pairs of eyes.

The Scorpion can pinch and sting
He's risky at both ends

But treat him well and learn his ways
And you can still be friends.

Scorpion mothers carry their babies on their backs.

S is for Scorpion

The patterns on a Tortoise shell are like fingerprints—every one is different.

The Tortoise shell
has sixty bones
A fact you
can't ignore

It must work well,
because some live
A hundred years
or more.

The oldest tortoises on record have lived to be about 200 years old.

Tortoises have strong jaws, but no teeth.

T is for Tortoise

The Umbrella Cockatoo is a parrot that loves attention and can live 50-75 years.

Extremely clever, Umbrella Cockatoos enjoy solving puzzles and learning tricks.

Mostly white on the outside, an Umbrella Cockatoo's under feathers can be yellow.

When Umbrella Cockatoo is calm
Her feathered crest is down

But when she's startled or annoyed
She lifts her royal crown.

U is for Umbrella Cockatoo

Veiled Chameleons get their name from the two-inch crest on their heads.

The Veiled Chameleon's
stripes and spots
Make this the reptile clown

Climbing high,
he hooks his tail
And dangles upside down.

A Veiled Chameleon's eyes move independently from one another.

All chameleons have long sticky tongues.

V is for Veiled Chameleon

White's Tree Frog is sometimes called the "dumpy tree frog" or "smiling tree frog".

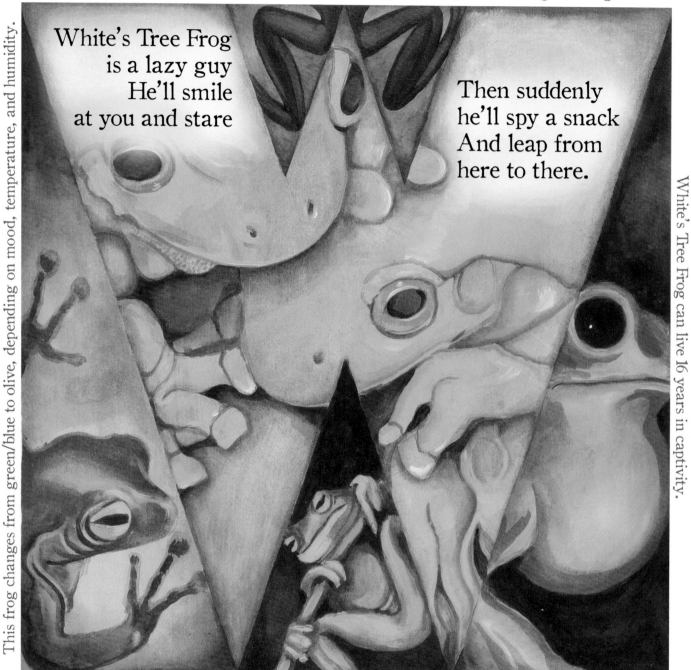

This frog changes from green/blue to olive, depending on mood, temperature, and humidity.

White's Tree Frog
is a lazy guy
He'll smile
at you and stare

Then suddenly
he'll spy a snack
And leap from
here to there.

White's Tree Frog can live 16 years in captivity.

W is for White's Tree Frog

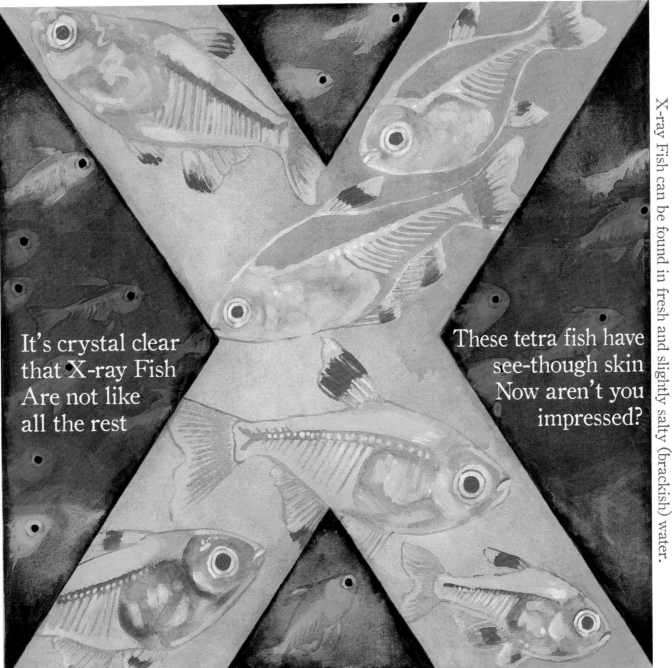

The X-ray tetra is also known as the golden pristella tetra.

Though often transparent, X-ray Fish can also be silver or yellow.

X-ray Fish can be found in fresh and slightly salty (brackish) water.

It's crystal clear
that X-ray Fish
Are not like
all the rest

These tetra fish have
see-though skin
Now aren't you
impressed?

X is for X-ray Fish

Yellow-bellied Sliders come out of the water to bask, soaking up light and heat.

This turtle is named for its yellow and black lower shell.

Yellow-bellied Sliders are omnivores, which means they eat vegetation and meat.

The Yellow-bellied Slider sits along the water's rim

Basking calmly on a log before he takes a swim.

Y is for Yellow-bellied Slider

Male Zebra Finches learn to sing from their fathers or other males.

Male Zebra Finches have orange cheeks and red beaks.

Female Zebra Finches have gray cheeks and orange beaks.

Zebra finches have bright beaks
And tails striped white and black

But only males learn to sing
They seem to have the knack.

Z is for Zebra Finch

When looking for some things to do
Next ho-hum afternoon
The animals all hope that you'll
Come back and visit soon.